Science - Just
Add Salt

Science - Just Add Salt

by Sandra Markle
Illustrated by June Otani

SCHOLASTIC
New York Toronto London Auckland Sydney

No part of this publication may be reproduced in whole or in part, or stored in a retrieval system, or transmitted in any form or by any means, electronic, mechanical, photocopying, recording, or otherwise, without written permission of the publisher. For information regarding permission, write to Scholastic Inc., 555 Broadway, New York, NY 10012.

ISBN 0-590-46537-6

Text copyright © 1994 by Sandra Markle.
Illustrations copyright © 1994 by Scholastic Inc.
All rights reserved. Published by Scholastic Inc.

12 11 10 9 8 7 6 5 4 3 2 1   4 5 6 7 8 9/9

Printed in the U.S.A.   40

First Scholastic printing, March 1994

Contents

Can you separate salt from salt water?
Can you use salt to make water stack up
  in layers as if by magic?
Can you get a drink of fresh water when
  only salt water is available?

Yes, you can do all this and more! All you
need are some materials you will find at home
or can purchase cheaply at a grocery or
hobby store — and salt. Then perform the
activities in this book to find out how science
can help you do some exciting things, especially with a dash of salt.

Along the way, you'll discover why salt is essential for animals and people to be healthy. You'll also discover where salt comes from and how it gets to your saltshaker. There will be quizzes and some challenges to keep you thinking, too, as you discover some amazing facts about salt.

Remember

- Do not do any activity involving a flame or a hot stove without an adult to help you.

- Clean up the work area after you finish your project.

- Have fun!

Check Out Different Kinds of Salt

Salt is a mineral. When you think of salt, you probably think of table salt. But there are other kinds. Take a closer look at three kinds of salt.

You'll need:

3 tablespoons of each of these salts —
   Common table salt
   Any "lite" salt or salt substitute
     (Check the ingredient list to
      be sure it's potassium nitrate.)
   Epsom salt
Water

A sheet of black construction paper
A magnifying glass
3 clear glasses or plastic cups
A measuring cup
Measuring spoons
A spoon

Put a few crystals of each of the three salts
on the black paper. Look at the crystals with
the magnifying glass. In what ways are the
crystals alike? How are they different?

Rub a finger over each type of salt. Does
one crumble more easily than another?

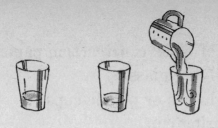

Next, pour ¼ cup of cold tap water into each glass.

Add three teaspoons of table salt to the first glass. Stir, timing how long it takes for the crystals to completely dissolve.

When the crystals are dissolved, the salt will seem to disappear. That's because the salt molecules are completely mixed with the water molecules.

Rinse and dry the spoon.

Repeat, adding three teaspoons of salt substitute to the second glass.

Finally, add three teaspoons of Epsom salt to the third glass.

Did you discover that the crystals of table salt look like cubes? Even very tiny crystals of table salt have this shape. That's because table salt is made up of an equal number of sodium and chlorine atoms. When these atoms bond together to form salt, the structure they form is in the shape of a cube.

How would you describe the shape of the crystals of Epsom salt and salt substitute?

When you mix the salts in water, the one with the smallest crystals dissolves fastest. What other tests can you think of to try to find out how these three salts are alike and how they are different? You might compare the color. Which appears clearest? Taste a little of each. Can you tell which is which?

Make Salt Dough Art

You'll need to use the stove, so ask an adult to be your partner and work with you on this activity.

When you add salt to a flour-and-water dough, you will be able to create sculptures that will last.

To mix some up, you'll need:

1 cup flour
½ cup salt
1 teaspoon
  cream of tartar
1 cup water
1 tablespoon oil
A metal spoon

A saucepan
A potholder
A cooling rack
A metal cookie sheet
A sheet of waxed paper
Food coloring (optional)

Pour the flour, salt, and cream of tartar into the pan. Stir in the water and oil. Add food coloring if you want the dough to be colored. Mix well.

Cook over medium heat, stirring until a thick dough forms. Use the potholder to move the pan to the cooling rack.

Let the dough sit until it is cool — about 20 or 30 minutes.

Place the dough on the metal cookie sheet as you work. Shape the dough into any shape you want. Make one big sculpture or lots of small ones. Transfer the finished shapes to the sheet of waxed paper. Let the dough dry to harden. (It will take several days.)

To add more color, you can paint the sculpture with acrylic paints. For an attractive shine and additional protection, coat the dried sculpture with a high-gloss shellac.

Store any unused dough in a self-sealing plastic bag at room temperature. Squeeze out any extra air and keep the bag tightly zipped shut. The dough will stay soft and ready to use for weeks.

Salt Power

Have you ever seen these words on the label of an electric hair dryer or shaver: "DO NOT USE IN A SHOWER OR BATH."

Have you ever been told to get out of a swimming pool because of lightning in the area?

Why all this caution?

It's because water conducts electricity, meaning water lets charged particles called electrons pass through it easily. Salt water is an even better conductor of electricity. This activity will let you safely see that for yourself.

You'll need:

A small piece of aluminum foil, at least 10
 inches long and 3 inches wide
Clear tape, ½ inch wide
Scissors
A flashlight with a 2.5-volt bulb
 and 2 D-cell batteries
 (Test it to see that it works.)
A spoon
Table salt
Water
2 bowls

Make Your Own Electrical System

First make two "wires" out of the aluminum foil and the clear tape. To do this, turn
the aluminum foil so that the dull side is up.
Pull out two strips of tape about 10 inches
long and stick them on the foil about an inch
apart. Cut out the strips and fold each in half
lengthwise with the tape on the inside.

Now take the two batteries out of the flashlight. (Set the bulb end aside.) Put one battery on top of the other with the knob end of one against the flat end of the other. Tape the batteries together at the middle.

You are ready now to test your electrical system! Set the flat end of the stacked batteries on one of the foil wires. Wrap the other end of this wire around the screw base of the bulb. Then touch the metal tip of the bulb's base to the knob end of the top battery.

You've now created a complete circuit, meaning that electricity is able to flow out of the battery, through the wire to the bulb, and back to the battery. The bulb will light. If it doesn't, check your connections.

Once you know your circuit works and will light the bulb, fill both bowls three-quarters full of water. Add salt to one bowl until it stops dissolving. You have created a super-saturated solution.

Watch the Bulb Light Up!

Set the flat end of the stacked batteries on one of the wires, and place the free end of that wire in the fresh water. Place one end of the other wire in this water, too. Be sure that the two wires are close together but *not* touching.

Wrap the free end of the second wire around the bulb's screw base and touch the metal tip of the base to the knob end of the battery. You probably won't see the light glow, but if it does, it will be faint.

Now, swing the free ends of each wire out of the fresh water and into the salt water. Put them close together but not touching. You'll see the salt water start to fizzle around the end of the wire attached to the battery. The bulb lights up!

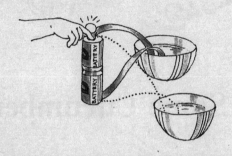

Why?

The current was conducted from molecule to molecule through the salty water. The fizz happens because water is made up of atoms of hydrogen and oxygen. When the electric current passes through the salt water, some of the water breaks down, releasing hydrogen gas at the battery end and oxygen gas at the light bulb end.

If the bulb does not light up in the salt water, try adding some more salt.

Salt Some Cucumbers

Today we preserve foods mainly by chilling and freezing them. Before it was easy and affordable to refrigerate, salting was an important way to keep foods from spoiling. But how does salt change foods? Find out for yourself.

You'll need:

2 soup bowls
A measuring cup
Measuring spoons

6 nearly identical slices of cucumber,
     each about as thick as a fifty-cent piece
     (You may want to ask an adult partner
     to do this for you.)
Water
Salt

Pour ½ cup of cool tap water into each bowl.
Add two teaspoons of salt to one and stir
until the crystals are completely dissolved.

Arrange three cucumber slices in each bowl, spacing so that they don't overlap.

After 30 minutes, remove the slices. Bend them back and forth. The slices that were in salty water will be limper. That's because the cucumber lost some water. The water in the cucumber's cells moved out of the cucumber and into the salty water.

This "drying" process doesn't leave the cucumbers completely flat and shriveled the way air drying would, but it's enough to discourage mold growth.

Salt is also a mild antiseptic, meaning that it kills bacteria that could cause foods to spoil.

Who Needs Salt?

Today, some people are concerned about eating salty foods. But does your body need salt to be healthy? Take this quiz to find out the facts. The results may surprise you.

1. You need to eat some salt every day to be healthy. True or false?

2. It's impossible to know if there is a lot of salt in a can of soup. True or false?

3. You need less salt when you're going to be active outdoors on a hot summer day. True or false?

4. Eating very salty food may make you feel puffy. True or false?

5. It's good to eat salt to which iodine has been added. True or false?

1. *You need to eat some salt every day to be healthy. True or false?* True. Both humans and animals need salt in their diets to be healthy. In fact, adults need about 6 grams — or a thimbleful — a day, and children need about half as much.

The body needs salt for the nerves and brain to function successfully. Salt is also needed to maintain a proper balance between the fluid portion of the blood and the number of molecules dissolved in it. Without this balance, the body's cells would absorb too much water and burst. So the body tries to maintain a certain concentration of salt in water.

2. *It's impossible to know if there is a lot of salt in a can of soup. True or false?* False. You can tell how much salt is in a can of soup or in any packaged food by checking the list of ingredients. The ingredients are listed in order, depending on the amount used to prepare the food. So whatever there is the most of in the food product is listed first; the one that makes up the next biggest part of the food product is listed second; and so forth. Salt should definitely *not* be the first ingredient on the list, or even in the top five.

3. *You need less salt when you're going to be active outdoors on a hot summer day. True or false?* False. Some salt is lost every day by excreting urine and by sweating. If you sweat a lot on a hot day, you need to eat something salty to help make up for this increased loss.

4. *Eating very salty food may make you feel puffy. True or false?* True. When you eat very salty food or a lot of salty food, your body will retain water in an effort to regain a balance.

5. *It's good to eat salt to which iodine has been added. True or false?* True. Iodine is needed by the body's thyroid gland, which is located in the neck. This gland produces special chemicals that control many of the body's functions.

Normally, fresh vegetables take in iodine from the soil, and eating those vegetables supplies the body with iodine. Years ago, though, research scientists learned that iodine isn't equally available in the soil throughout all parts of the world, so some people don't get enough iodine from their foods. Since most people add some salt to foods, iodine was added to salt as it was prepared for packaging.

Some of the tiny crystals in table salt are actually tiny crystals of iodine — just enough to keep the body healthy.

Take the Salt Out of Salt Water

As long as the earth has salty oceans, there won't ever be a lack of salt. In fact, you can get salt as easily as any industrial salt producer can once you know the science for extracting salt from salt water.

You'll need:

A glass pie plate
Salt
Water
A tall drinking glass
A measuring cup
A spoon

Fill the tall glass about three-quarters full with warm water. Dump in about ¼ cup of salt and stir until the crystals are dissolved. The water is now very salty. If you want to be sure, dip a clean finger into the water and lick it off to check for a salty taste.

Next, pour the salty water into the pie plate and set it in a warm, sunny location. Check it every day. You'll notice that the water level slowly shrinks. Within a few days, the water will completely disappear. What's left behind is a sparkling crust of salt crystals on the bottom of the pie plate.

This happened because the water evaporated. As the water molecules came in contact with the air, their movement increased. The faster they moved, the more the molecules bumped into each other and moved farther apart. When they were moving fast enough to spread far apart, the water changed to a gas called water vapor, which was carried away by the air.

Salt is made up of sodium and chlorine atoms. When the salt was dissolved in water, these atoms separated. As the water evaporated, however, the atoms bonded together again to form salt crystals.

What you've just done is a method that's been used since ancient times to extract salt from seawater. In fact, to speed up the process, salt water was often boiled. With an adult partner's help, you can try this, too, mixing up salt water as before and then boiling it in a pan. The steam you'll see rising from the pan will be the water vapor. Remove the pan to a cooling rack as soon as the last of the water has evaporated. The crust left behind on the bottom of the pan is salt. If you'd like, you could crumble this salt and use it to season your food.

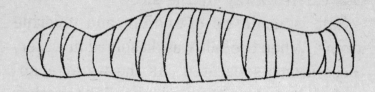

Save It Egyptian Style

Have you ever seen pictures of an ancient Egyptian mummy? Long ago, the Egyptians preserved their pharaohs and other rich people by using a special chemical called natron, which dried the body's tissues after death and kept them from decaying.

Just as you found salt crystals remaining after salt water evaporated, the ancient Egyptians collected natron as a crusty material left behind when inland seas evaporated. But you can mix up several familiar chemicals to create natron and see how this ancient embalming process works for yourself. The recipe for natron was supplied by the Denver Museum of Natural History.

You'll need:

A small mixing bowl
½ cup baking soda
½ cup all-fabric dry powdered bleach whose main ingredient is sodium carbonate
¼ cup salt
A spoon
¼ of an apple

Mix the baking soda, bleach, and salt together in the bowl, stirring well. What you've created is natron. Bury the quarter apple in the natron, making sure it's completely covered.

To completely mummify the apple will take about a week, but check the apple after two days. Check again after four days. Does it surprise you to see how much moisture the apple has lost? Of course, being buried in plain salt would remove moisture. Natron, though, will also break down fats and oils; plain salt can't do that.

According to an ancient Greek named Herodotus who visited Egypt and wrote about his discoveries, the process of embalming a body took about 70 days. The wrappings were added after the body was removed from the natron. Egypt has a hot, dry, desert climate. How do you think this climate affected the embalming process?

A Salty Problem

You've discovered how to extract salt from salt water, but do you know you can also separate salt from sand?

Pour ½ cup of table salt and ½ cup of clean sand into a self-sealing plastic bag. Seal and shake. Then see if you can figure out a way to separate the sand and salt once again.

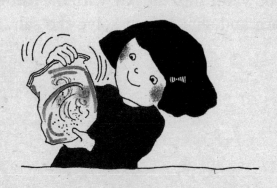

To solve this problem, start by brainstorming — thinking of all the possible things you might try. Make a list of at least five of your best ideas. Then look over your list, considering for what reasons, if any, each one might not work. Also think about what equipment you'd need to use. And be sure it's something you have on hand or that's inexpensive and easy to obtain.

Choose the one idea you think is the most likely to successfully separate the sand and salt. Then collect what you need to use and test your idea before reading on. One solution follows, but you may come up with another that works just as well.

You'll remember that as salty water evaporates, the salt is left behind. So pour a cup of water into the bag with the salt-sand mixture and shake to dissolve the salt.

Next, place a cone-shaped coffee filter in a glass. Ask a friend to hold the ends. Slowly pour the sandy salt water into the filter.

The sand will pile up in the filter, but the water will flow out into the glass. Slowly lift the filter, letting any remaining water drain out. Then pour the salty water into a pie plate.

When the water has evaporated, the salt will be left behind, and the salt and sand will be separate once again.

Stack Water

The saltier water is, the denser, or thicker, it is. Less salty water will actually "float" atop saltier water. You can do an experiment to prove it.

You'll need:

3 water glasses that hold at least
 two cups of water
Measuring spoons
A carton of salt
A measuring cup
Blue, red, and yellow food coloring
A spoon
Water

Pour one cup cool tap water into one tall glass. Pour in two tablespoons of salt, stirring until nearly all of the salt has dissolved. Now pour half of this super-salty water into the second tall glass. Add blue food coloring to make the water bright blue.

Pour half a cup of water into the remaining salt water. Stir and add enough yellow food coloring to make the water bright yellow.

Pour a cup of water into the remaining glass.

Add a few drops of red food coloring.

Wait five minutes to let the water in each glass stop moving after you stirred it. Next, spoon the yellow-colored water onto the surface of the blue water. Work slowly, letting the water just slip off the spoon. Because the water is less salty, the yellow water will float on top of the blue water. It's impossible, though, not to stir up the water slightly during this process. This will create a green layer on top of the saltier blue water.

Finally, spoon the unsalty red water on top of the green water. Again some mixing will occur, making this top layer appear brownish-red. Look at the three distinct layers through the side of the glass.

After a few hours, salt that wasn't dissolved will settle to the bottom of the glass and the water layers will become clearer. As long as the water isn't stirred or jiggled too much, the colored layers will stay stacked for quite a while — even as long as several days.

Keep checking to see how long your salt water layers stay stacked. Eventually, the salt molecules will migrate from where there's a lot to where there's less, and the layers will begin to blend together.

What do you think would happen if you tried to spoon the denser blue water onto the less-salty yellow water? Mix up another set of the salty solutions and test your prediction.

Now, use what you discovered about water density to tackle this new challenge. Normally, a hard-boiled egg will sink to the bottom when you put it in a quart jar nearly full of water. Can you use what you discovered about salt water's increased density to make a hard-boiled egg float halfway between the top and the bottom of the jar?

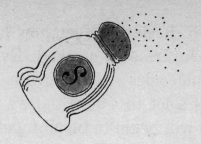

Shake Out Some Salt

Want to know where salt comes from before it gets to your saltshaker? Then check out these facts.

- In ancient times, people who lived near the ocean collected salt by throwing seawater on blazing logs. The water quickly turned to steam, leaving a crust of salt behind on the wood. (Of course, you had to like a little ash with your salt.) Later, salt water was boiled in kettles to evaporate the water and collect the salt. Today, big tanks are used to do this job.

- In Utah, very salty water from Great Salt Lake is pumped through a series of shallow ponds each covering from 15 to 90 acres. In this hot, desert climate, the water evaporates and a thick layer of salt builds up on the pond floor. When very little water remains, it's pumped back into the lake. The salt — as much as 400 tons of it — is scraped up and stored until it can be washed, dried, screened, and then ground up.

- In many different parts of the world, salt is mined from deposits of rock salt that were left behind when ancient seas dried up. Although it's no longer in operation, one such salt mine lies under Detroit, Michigan. It was once among the largest salt mines in the world.

- Salt is still being deposited today. In the Andes Mountains in Chile, for example, salt basins are slowly evaporating, leaving behind thick layers of salt.

Get a Drink of Water the Hard Way

While three-quarters of the earth is covered with water, 97 percent of all that available water is salty. People can't drink salt water, though. The salt causes water to diffuse out of their body's cells and they die. So in places where fresh water is especially scarce, people have developed methods for extracting fresh water from salt water. Once you discover the basics in this activity, you'll be able to do that yourself. It's something to keep in mind if you're ever stranded on a desert island.

You'll need:

A small juice glass or plastic cup
Table salt
Warm water

A tablespoon or soup spoon
A clean, large, self-sealing plastic bag

Fill the cup nearly full of warm water and stir in two spoonfuls of salt until it's completely dissolved. (You could use cool water, but heat speeds up the molecules and makes the salt dissolve faster.) Dip a clean finger into the cup of water and lick it to prove to yourself that it tastes salty.

Slide the cup inside the bag, seal, and place in a warm, sunny place. Check in a couple of hours. The inside of the bag will look fogged. You may even see tiny droplets of water. When the sun sets, you should see large droplets of water clinging to the plastic.

Be sure your hands are clean and dry. Then open the bag, wipe your finger through the droplets, and lick it.

Did it surprise you that the water on your finger didn't taste salty? Now, dip your finger into the cup again and lick it to prove to yourself that this water is still salty.

You wouldn't normally put anything from an experiment into your mouth, but in this case, since you only used table salt and water, it was okay to do so. The sun's heat simply set up a water cycle similar to the one that occurs in nature to separate the water and salt. The droplets you saw on the inside of the bag formed as the water in the cup evaporated or changed to water vapor, rose, and then condensed or changed back into a liquid when it cooled.

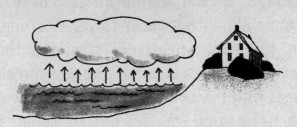

Clouds form over the ocean because
the water that evaporates cools as it rises into
the atmosphere.

The rain that falls from
these clouds is fresh water because most of
the dissolved salt is left behind when salt
water evaporates.

Turning Salt Water into Fresh Water

One of the most common desalting methods
is to force large amounts of salt water

through special membranes. These membranes allow the water to pass through but not the salt, effectively straining the salt water. Before this technique was developed, fresh water was collected from salt water in much the same way you did, by boiling it and collecting the salt-free steam which was then allowed to condense.

Either method of desalting salt water requires a lot of energy and so it's an expensive process. On a desert island like Aruba, which has no natural fresh water supply, it's the only answer.

You might think that solar energy would be a cheap source of energy for this process. But solar processors only work when the sun shines, and they tend to have problems with the growth of algae that contaminate the water.

Undoubtedly, as cities like Los Angeles, California, have an ever greater need and a dwindling supply of fresh water, new efforts will be made to find an inexpensive way to use the oceans as a resource.

The Truth About Salt — Maybe

Want to know some fascinating facts about salt? Then take this quiz.

1. Salt has always been cheap. True or false?

2. Over time, salt deposits in the earth will change shape and move. True or false?

3. All animals need salt, but none are able to drink salt water. True or false?

4. Salt is actually made up of two poisonous chemicals. True or false?

5. The oceans are salty due to the natural weathering, or breakdown, of the earth's rocks. True or false?

1. *Salt has always been cheap. True or false?* False. In ancient times, salt was so hard to come by that it was greatly valued. Roman soldiers received part of their pay in *sal* (the Latin word for salt). In fact, that's the origin of the world *salary*, meaning what a person gets paid for doing work. It's also the origin of the saying that someone is "worth his salt."

Cities like Timbuktu, in Mali, a country in northwestern Africa, and Venice, Italy, gained wealth and power partly because they were centers of the salt trade. As recently as just before World War II, salt was stored in banks in Ethiopia and considered part of that African country's financial wealth.

Salt has become easily obtainable and inexpensive only in recent times.

2. *Over time, salt deposits in the earth will change shape and move. True or false?* True. When under pressure, deep down underground, deposits of salt will slowly deform, or "creep." In fact, inside salt mines there are constant snapping, crackling sounds as the rock salt shifts in response to the weight of overlaying layers. Daily checks are made to be sure the roof of a salt mine tunnel isn't creeping downward at a rate that could become a threat to equipment and workers.

3. *All animals need salt, but none are able to drink salt water. True or false?* False. A few animals, such as the marine iguana of the Galápagos Islands, have special salt glands that let their bodies extract and eliminate excess salt. These animals can get the water they need by drinking salt water. They get rid of the excess salt by blowing brine (very salty water) out through their nostrils.

4. *Salt is actually made up of two poisonous chemicals. True or false?* True. Both sodium and chlorine, the two chemicals that combine to form table salt, are poisonous. When they combine to form salt, however, they're harmless and edible.

Today, numerous chemical industries have sprung from the ability to separate sodium and chlorine from salt. These chemicals are then used as they are, or become ingredients in other products. Chlorine, for example, is essential for keeping drinking water pure and swimming pools clean. It's also used to bleach paper and to produce explosives, dry-cleaning fluids, and insecticides.

5. *The oceans are salty due to the natural weathering, or breakdown, of the earth's rocks. True or false?* True. The seas are salty because sodium and chloride molecules are easily dissolved from rocks and soil. Water running off after a rain carries these molecules into streams, rivers, and eventually into the ocean.

When this natural flow of water toward the sea is altered, such as when rivers are dammed, the stored water becomes much saltier than normal. This is what's happening in the southwestern United States due to dams being built along the Colorado River. The water being used for irrigation has a higher concentration of salt than usual and is causing salt to build up in the soil. This, in turn, is leading to serious problems because plants don't grow well in salty soils.

Do a Little Salt Magic

Tell your family and friends that you can lift an ice cube with a piece of thread. Here's how you can use a little science magic to perform that trick.

You'll need:

An ice cube
12 inches of thread
Table salt

Wet one end of the thread and coil the wet end on top of the ice cube. Sprinkle salt over the cube, covering the thread. Hold onto the other end of the thread.

After about a minute, pull up the thread. Keep pulling when the string becomes taut and you'll be able to lift the ice cube.

What's happening is that the salt melts the surface of the ice. However, melting takes heat, and that heat comes from the surrounding air and even from the wet thread. In fact, the melting ice takes enough heat from the water on the thread to make it freeze, forming an ice glaze. The ice glaze sticks the thread to the cube's surface so that your gentle tug can lift it.

Whip Up Some Sherbet

Now use what you've learned about salt making ice melt to make a tasty sherbet treat.

You'll need:

A large metal bowl
A smaller metal bowl that fits inside the large bowl. It's best if this bowl has tall, straight sides. (You can substitute a small metal saucepan.)
Crushed ice
Rock salt
A measuring cup
A soup spoon
A long-handled iced-tea spoon
A paper towel
A plastic garbage bag
½ cup carbonated orange-flavored soft drink
¼ cup sweetened condensed milk

Cover your work area with the plastic garbage bag. Pour the soft drink and sweetened milk into the small bowl, stirring to mix well.

Scoop enough crushed ice into the large bowl to cover the bottom and sprinkle on rock salt with the soup spoon.

Place the small bowl on the ice. Pack crushed ice around the bowl until it comes halfway up the sides. Spoon on more rock salt, being careful not to get any of the crystals in the orange mixture.

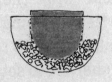 

Add more ice to about two inches below the rim of the small bowl and spoon on more rock salt.

Turn the bowls using two different motions: 1) hold on to the rim of the bigger bowl and turn it around and around the smaller inner bowl; 2) hold on to the rim of the smaller bowl, rocking it back and forth as you turn it around inside the bigger bowl. Every few minutes, stir the mixture with the long-handled spoon. (Lay the spoon on the paper towel between stirs.)

In just a few minutes, you will find the orange mixture will begin to freeze along the edge. Scoop this out to taste what the finished sherbet will be like. Keep turning the bowl and stirring. It will take about 15 to 20 minutes for the soft frozen sherbet to set up.

Make Metal Rust

You'll be using a stove, so ask an adult partner to work with you on this activity.

In the winter, you often see trucks out salting the roads to melt the snow and ice. But salt isn't the perfect solution for treating icy roads.

For example, when salt soaks into concrete roads that are reinforced with steel rods, it creates an especially dangerous problem on bridges. When metal rusts, the structure of the metal changes and weakens. A metal bridge that rusts can support less weight; it may become too weak to use.

Rust forms when certain metals, especially iron, come in contact with the oxygen

in the air. But how does salt effect rusting?
Check it out.

You'll need:

3 plastic cups
Enough steel wool to make 3 balls, each
    about the size of a quarter
Salt
Water
A measuring cup
A saucepan with a lid
A potholder
A cooling rack
Masking tape
A marking pen
Clear wrap

Put a strip of tape on each of the cups and
number them 1, 2, and 3.

Put one ball of steel wool into cup 1 and set it aside.

Now pour two cups of water into the pan and heat until it boils. (Boiling removes much of the oxygen from the water.) Remove the pan from the stove with the potholder. Cover and let sit on the cooling rack for two hours or until the water is completely cool.

Pour some of the boiled water into cups 2 and 3. Add a teaspoon of salt to cup 3. Place one ball of steel wool in each cup and cover cups 2 and 3 with clear wrap to keep oxygen from naturally entering the water.

Check the steel wool every day for spots that look rusted. The wet steel wool will rust more quickly than the steel wool that's only exposed to the air. But does being wet and salty make it rust even faster?

Many cities have discovered that after years of salt soaking into concrete roads, the steel reinforcements in the road have rusted. The rusted steel actually takes up more space than the unrusted steel, so the pavement becomes broken and has to be repaired.